HAL•LEONARD

VIOLIN
PLAY•ALONG

CLASSICAL TREASURES

CONTENTS

ISBN 978-1-4584-1952-1

HAL•LEONARD®
CORPORATION
7777 W. BLUEMOUND RD. P.O. BOX 13819 MILWAUKEE, WI 53213

In Australia Contact:
Hal Leonard Australia Pty. Ltd.
4 Lentara Court
Cheltenham, Victoria, 3192 Australia
Email: ausadmin@halleonard.com.au

Visit Hal Leonard Online at
www.halleonard.com

Air on the G String

from Suite in D (BWV 1068)

By Johann Sebastian Bach (1685-1750)

Anitra's Dance

from Peer Gynt Suite, Op. 46

By Edvard Grieg (1843-1907)

3

Arioso

from Cantata 'Ich steh' mit einem Fuß im Grabe' (BWV 156)
By Johann Sebastian Bach (1685-1750)

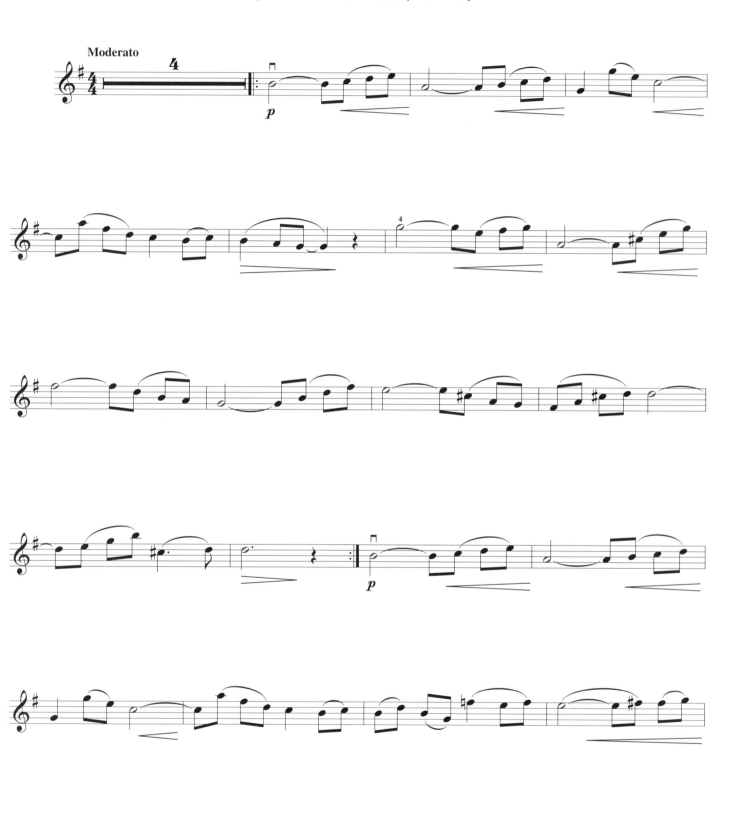

Ave Maria

based on Prelude No. 1 from 'Das Wohltemperierte Klavier I' (BWV 846)

By Johann Sebastian Bach (1685-1750)/Charles Gounod (1818-1893)

Elegy

from Lyric Pieces II, Op. 38 No. 6
By Edvard Grieg (1843-1907)

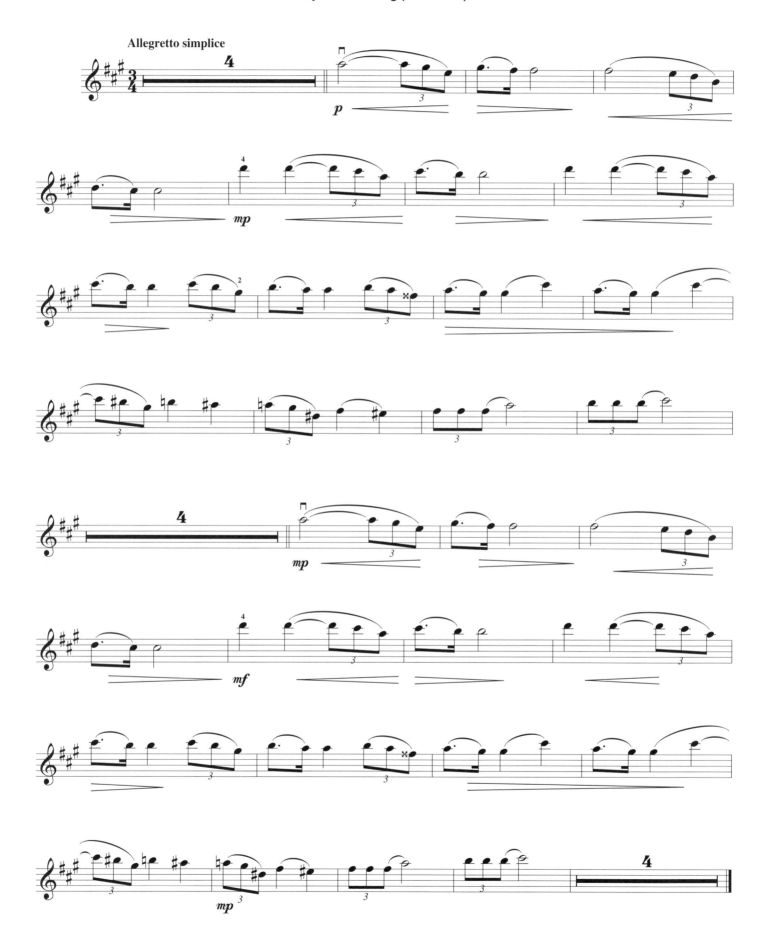

Largo

from Xerxes (HWV 40)
By George Frideric Handel (1685-1759)

Hornpipe

from Water Music Suite No. I, F major (HWV 348)
By George Frideric Handel (1685-1759)

8

Last Spring

from Elegiac Melodies, Op. 34 No. 2
By Edvard Grieg (1843-1907)

March

from The Magic Flute (KV 620)
By Wolfgang Amadeus Mozart (1756-1791)

Allegro moderato

Minuetto

from Sonata for Piano and Violin (KV 6)
By Wolfgang Amadeus Mozart (1756-1791)

A Musical Joke

Movement 4 (KV 522)
By Wolfgang Amadeus Mozart (1756-1791)

Sarabande

from Suite for Harpsichord (HWV 437)
By George Frideric Handel (1685-1759)